Bacteria Timeline

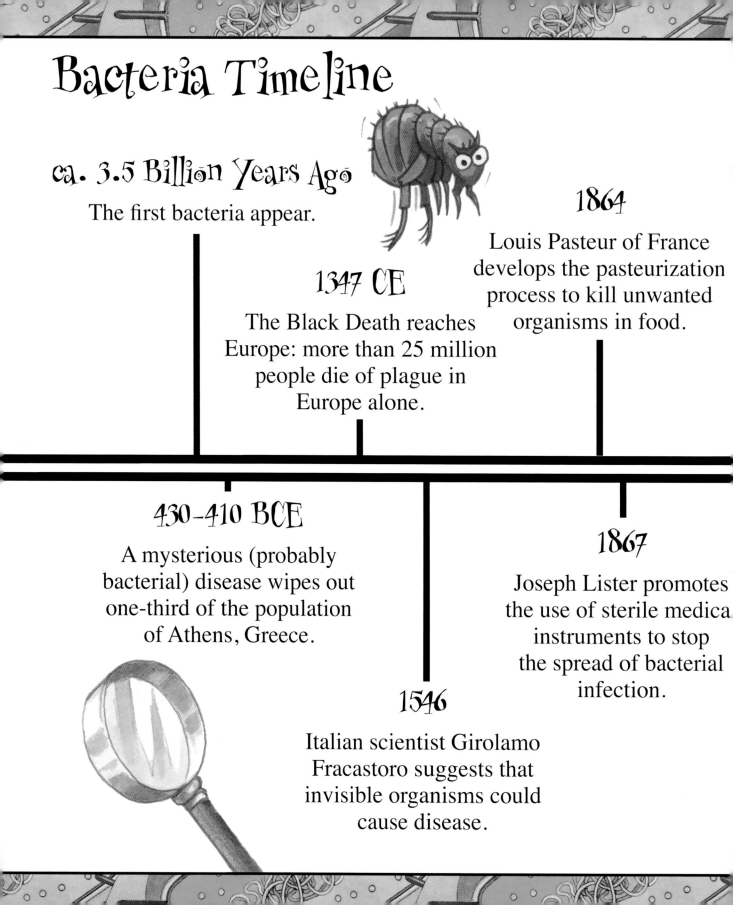

ca. 3.5 Billion Years Ago

The first bacteria appear.

1347 CE

The Black Death reaches Europe: more than 25 million people die of plague in Europe alone.

1864

Louis Pasteur of France develops the pasteurization process to kill unwanted organisms in food.

430–410 BCE

A mysterious (probably bacterial) disease wipes out one-third of the population of Athens, Greece.

1867

Joseph Lister promotes the use of sterile medical instruments to stop the spread of bacterial infection.

1546

Italian scientist Girolamo Fracastoro suggests that invisible organisms could cause disease.

1888

Dutch scientist Martinus Beijerinck studies the process of nitrogen fixation.

1928

Scottish scientist Alexander Fleming discovers and observes penicillin, the first truly successful antibiotic.

2014

Canadian scientists find the first antibiotic-resistant bacteria in a food source (raw squid).

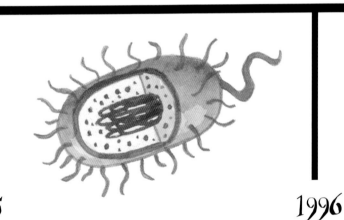

1905

Robert Koch of Germany receives the Nobel Prize for identifying bacteria as the cause of tuberculosis.

1996

More than 10,000 people die in an outbreak of bacterial meningitis in West Africa.

Putting Bacteria to Work

Cutaway view of a compost maker

Air

Garden waste
Include: leaves, grass cuttings, fallen fruit
Don't include: *twigs, branches*

Worms feed on organic matter and their waste is passed out as casts—nutrient-rich, fine material that also contains useful bacteria.

Kitchen waste
Include: apple cores, fruit and vegetable peelings, eggshells
Don't include: *meat, fish, bones*

Paper and cardboard (torn into small pieces), sawdust, wood shavings

Bacteria in nearby soil are attracted to the organic matter, which they break down into carbohydrates and proteins. These can be broken down further to release essential nutrients that are good for garden plants.

Water

For more information, see pages 22–23.

Some people think of compost as a living organism in its own right. In many ways it is, thanks to the bacteria that break down the ingredients. The bacteria most useful for composting need a good supply of air and water to do their work, and, just like you, they thrive on a balanced diet. For them it's a balance of nitrogen and carbon. Nitrogen comes from fresh "green" ingredients such as food scraps (not meat or bones) and grass clippings. "Brown" ingredients—long-dead materials such as dried leaves and shredded newspaper—add the carbon. Too much grass, though, can block the air supply and smother the bacteria.

Author:

Roger Canavan is an accomplished author who has written, edited, and contributed to more than a dozen books about science and other educational subjects. His three children are his sternest critics—and his fellow explorers in the pursuit of knowledge.

Artist:

Mark Bergin was born in Hastings, England, in 1961. He studied at Eastbourne College of Art and has specialized in historical reconstructions as well as aviation and maritime subjects since 1983. He lives in Bexhill-on-Sea, England, with his wife and three children.

Series creator:

David Salariya was born in Dundee, Scotland. He has illustrated a wide range of books and has created and designed many new series for publishers in the UK and overseas. David established The Salariya Book Company in 1989. He lives in Brighton, England, with his wife, illustrator Shirley Willis, and their son, Jonathan.

Editors: **Stephen Haynes, Caroline Coleman**

Editorial Assistant: **Mark Williams**

PAPER FROM
SUSTAINABLE
FORESTS

Published in Great Britain in 2015 by
The Salariya Book Company Ltd
25 Marlborough Place, Brighton BN1 1UB

ISBN-13: 978-0-531-21363-6 (lib. bdg.) 978-0-531-21406-0 (pbk.)

All rights reserved.
Published in 2015 in the United States
by Franklin Watts
An imprint of Scholastic Inc.
Published simultaneously in Canada.

A CIP catalog record for this book is available from the Library of Congress.

Printed and bound in Heyuan, China.
Printed on paper from sustainable sources.
Reprinted in MMXIX.
4 5 6 7 8 9 10 R 24 23 22 21 20 19

You Wouldn't Want to Live Without™
Bacteria!

Written by
Roger Canavan

Illustrated by
Mark Bergin

Created and designed by
David Salariya

Franklin Watts®
An Imprint of Scholastic Inc.
NEW YORK • TORONTO • LONDON • AUCKLAND • SYDNEY
MEXICO CITY • NEW DELHI • HONG KONG
DANBURY, CONNECTICUT

Contents

Introduction

They are far too small to be seen with the naked eye, but bacteria are one of the most widespread forms of life. (We normally use the word *bacteria*, which is plural, because it's hard to imagine just one of them on its own; a loner is called a *bacterium*).

People have known what bacteria are for only a few centuries, but have been using them without realizing it for much longer—especially to make flavorful foods. But once we learned a little about bacteria, we learned that they caused horrible diseases. It's only now that people are learning about all the "good" bacteria, helping you fight disease, enrich the soil, and even power your family car.

ALTHOUGH IT TAKES a powerful microscope to see bacteria, they're all around you—on the floor, in your hair, and in the air you breathe.

Bacteria Are Bad For You... Aren't They?

When you hear the word *bacteria*, what images come to mind? Bodies being carried from rickety wooden houses centuries ago? A crying child looking at his swollen, infected thumb? A notice on a singer's Web site saying that her concerts are canceled because of a throat infection? Many illnesses—ranging from deadly to annoying—are caused by the spread of bacteria. And that spread can be very fast and unnoticed. Is it any surprise that many household cleaners have the word *antibacterial* in big letters on their labels?

MOSQUITO NETS are used in hot countries to guard against harmful viruses carried by those insects. But these nets also protect people from ticks and fleas, which can transmit dangerous bacterial diseases such as Lyme disease and plague.

Mosquito

Deer tick

Flea

17th-century plague doctor

THE PLAGUE was a deadly disease that swept through Europe and Asia many times. The most famous outbreak, in the 1300s, is often known as the Black Death. We now know that the plague was caused by bacteria spread to humans by fleas.

INFECTION FROM BACTERIA can be very serious for an expectant mother and her child. That's why labels on dairy products and other foods spell out the risk of bacterial infection.

DIRTY WATER is a breeding ground for nasty microorganisms. The bacterium *Escherichia coli* (usually called *E. coli*) can cause severe stomach pains and even kidney failure.

UNTIL THE 19th CENTURY, nobody knew that bacteria caused certain illnesses. Even after this had been discovered, there was still no reliable way of combating these diseases. But doctors now have an effective weapon—antibiotics—to fight back at bacteria. Scottish scientist Alexander Fleming discovered penicillin, which later became the first really successful antibiotic medicine, in 1928.

How Did Bacteria Get a Bad Name?

Imagine how it must have felt to see people around you suddenly getting sick and suffering—and not know what had caused the illness or how to treat it.

For thousands of years, people blamed all sorts of things for sickness and poor health—bad luck, smelly air, the full moon—because they had no way of discovering the real cause.

We now know that bacteria are linked to killer diseases such as the Black Death (caused by the bacterium *Yersinia pestis*), as well as many less serious infections. Is it any wonder that we have come to fear bacteria and develop medicines against them? But we're also beginning to understand that not all bacteria are harmful—some of them actually help to fight disease.

> I call them "animalcules" (tiny animals).

MICROSCOPES were developed in the 1590s. For the first time, people could see objects that were much too small to observe with the naked eye. Antonie van Leeuwenhoek, a self-taught Dutch scientist, made his own microscope and in 1676 became the first person to observe and record bacteria in a drop of lake water. Other scientists soon began to wonder whether these tiny objects were linked to diseases.

You Can Do It!

Leeuwenhoek's microscope looked like a magnifying glass. You can make a simple version by twisting a piece of fine wire to make a loop the size of a pea. Dip the loop in water and you'll have a watery lens.

BEFORE ANTIBIOTICS, the family of a sick child could only watch, wait, and hope for a recovery. Many people died in childhood.

PHYSICIANS IN ANCIENT EGYPT treated wounds with honey, which really does protect against bacterial infection. The sugar in honey draws moisture out of and helps to kill the bacteria—though the Egyptians did not know this.

YOUR BODY'S OWN IMMUNE SYSTEM can often combat infections by itself. When it can't, antibiotics may help. But remember that antibiotics destroy only bacteria—if your illness is caused by a virus, antibiotics won't help.

HARMFUL BACTERIA in dairy products can be destroyed by pasteurization. This process is named after the French scientist Louis Pasteur, who noted that heating foods and drinks to a certain temperature will kill dangerous bacteria.

How Much Do We Know About Bacteria?

Bacteria are some of the oldest, simplest, and most widespread forms of life on Earth. The first bacteria developed about 3.5 billion years ago. Most bacteria are about one micron long—that's one-millionth of a meter. In other words, 25,000 bacteria lined up next to each other would take up about an inch (2.5 centimeters) of space.

Although they're tiny, Earth's bacteria weigh more than all of the planet's plants and animals put together. Some of them can live in very hot or cold conditions; others thrive on the ocean floor. As many as 100 trillion bacteria live in your body. Luckily, most of them are harmless or even helpful.

> That type of vent is called a "black smoker."

HYDROTHERMAL VENTS are cracks in the ocean floor. Bacteria are able to survive on the rocks next to these super-hot, high-pressure pumps, which resemble geysers or underwater volcanoes.

Submersible (miniature submarine) exploring a hydrothermal vent

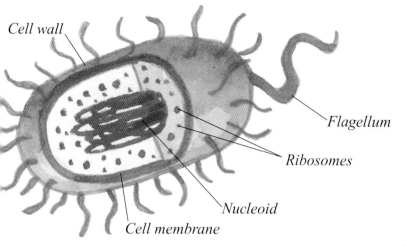

Cell wall

Flagellum

Ribosomes

Nucleoid

Cell membrane

BACTERIA come in many different shapes, but each one is made up of just one cell. The cell membrane and cell wall provide protection. The whiplike flagellum acts like a tail to propel the bacterium. Inside are the ribosomes, which produce essential proteins, and the nucleoid, which carries the DNA for reproduction.

How It Works

Like desert plants, some bacteria can survive in extreme conditions by becoming dormant for long periods of time. The bacterium releases an endospore, which contains DNA and ribosomes locked inside a tough coating. When conditions improve, the endospore breaks down and changes back into a bacterium.

Endospore   *Bacterium*

BACTERIA are constantly active in your body. If you swallow harmful bacteria, you'll soon begin to feel sick (left). Luckily, lots of helpful bacteria are also in your body to help you digest food and ward off illness.

DINOSAURS were not the earliest living things on Earth. When the first dinosaurs appeared, about 230 million years ago, bacteria had been around for more than 3 billion years.

GERM is a general word for all sorts of microbes that spread disease, such as fungi (which cause athlete's foot, left) and viruses, as well as bacteria.

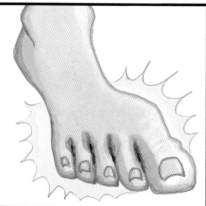

BACTERIA have even been to outer space. Several types of bacteria have "hitched rides" on astronauts' suits and equipment and blasted off.

Could You Live Without Bacteria?

Since bacteria have caused some of the deadliest diseases in history, you might think that the world would be a better place if we could get rid of them. Actually, most bacteria aren't bad at all. In fact, we all need bacteria—not just we humans, but all living things on Earth. Bacteria are constantly at work, keeping us well, getting rid of waste around us, helping the soil to remain productive for plants, and generally producing a balanced, healthy environment.

WITHOUT BACTERIA, dead things would pile up, smothering all chance of life. Bacteria lead the way in breaking down once-living things so that nutrients can return to the food cycle—and so that there is room for the rest of us.

YOUR BODY needs a constant supply of energy just to keep going, and even more to let you exercise or do your homework. You get that energy from the food you eat—but without the bacteria in your digestive system to break down that food, you would not get the energy that you need.

WITHOUT BACTERIA to act as a natural fertilizer, many crops just wouldn't grow. Certain bacteria in the soil use natural chemical processes to help plants find food to grow and remain healthy. And the plants that link up with bacteria spread that goodness to other plants.

You Can Do It!

Bacteria can wind up on your hands if you're preparing food or gardening. If you don't wash your hands properly, you spread bacteria to everything you touch. Take a look around your house, and write down all the places where bacteria can be deposited...and passed along.

IMAGINE if all foods tasted the same. Luckily, bacteria help give flavor to cheese, yogurt, salami, and lots of other foods.

DIARRHEA is no fun at all, and some cases can become serious. Luckily, bacteria are constantly at work in your digestive system to prevent it. Some even prevent the diarrhea caused by antibiotic medicines used to fight other bacteria.

YOUR BODY has ten times more bacteria cells than human cells. Luckily, most of those bacteria are helpful. Some of these "friendly" bacteria help fight diseases caused by parasites—invaders that feed off of your body. Some bacteria fight other bacteria. Conjunctivitis, an eye infection (above), is sometimes caused by bacteria.

Can Bacteria Be Tasty?

People have been cooking with bacteria for centuries—long before anyone had heard of bacteria. Some favorite foods depend on bacteria for their taste, texture, and look. The bacteria combine chemically with foods. For example, bacteria react with lactose, the natural sugar in milk, to produce lactic acid. As this acid builds up, the structure of the protein in the milk begins to change. This process is called curdling. It's the main change that helps create yogurt, and yogurt's tangy taste comes from the lactic acid. Early cooks did not know the science behind these bacterial foods, but they knew that something good was happening.

Dependable Food for Adventurers

GENGHIS KHAN'S fierce Mongol army relied on yogurt during its conquests of Asia and eastern Europe in the 13th century. Yogurt was easy to make and easy to carry on horseback.

MINERS in the 1849 California gold rush made sourdough bread, which depends on bacteria to help the dough rise. They'd save a bit of dough before baking and use it later to start the next batch.

THE STRINGY TEXTURE of mozzarella cheese owes a lot to bacteria that have reacted with milk. The chemical reaction needs just the right temperature and the right type of milk.

Top Tip

One study showed that kitchens contain 100,000 times more germs than bathrooms, so it's important to wash your hands thoroughly before and after you cook. Keep all your equipment clean, too.

CACAO BEANS—the raw ingredient used to make chocolate—taste nothing like chocolate until they have been fermented by bacteria.

THOSE HOLES that you see in Emmental and some other kinds of Swiss cheese are formed by carbon dioxide bubbles produced by the bacterium *Propionibacterium freudenreichii*.

HARMFUL BACTERIA can grow quickly if food isn't packaged or stored properly. A cracked or bulging can may contain the bacteria that cause botulism poisoning.

I'd better throw this away.

How Does Your Body Use Bacteria?

We've already seen that the "bad" bacteria that cause disease are outnumbered by "good" bacteria. Some of these good bacteria are medical superheroes. Your body uses them for defense, for recovery, and just to stay healthy.

Some of these bacteria are on duty in your mouth and nose, ready to fight off any attacks—including attacks from other bacteria. Others live in your stomach and intestines, helping you digest your food.

There are also bacteria guarding your health in the outside world. One type of bacteria can infect the mosquitoes that carry the deadly disease malaria. Mosquitoes affected by these bacteria bite the dust before they can bite you!

THE BACTERIA CELLS living inside your body outnumber your own body's cells by 10 to 1. Overall they weigh about 5 pounds (2.3 kilograms). That's as much as five 16-ounce (454-gram) jars of honey.

YOUR MOUTH WATERS when you see something tasty. Saliva contains chemicals called enzymes that team up with bacteria to start the process of digesting your food.

BACTERIA IN YOUR MOUTH are the body's first defense against many infections, such as colds. Fevers help "burn away" some of the bad bacteria causing an illness—just as dangerous bacteria in food can often be killed by cooking.

How It Works

Bacteria help cows to digest cellulose, the tough part of plants. The process produces a smelly gas called methane, which cows get rid of... just as you get rid of gas when you've digested some foods. Some scientists blame cow methane for part of the problem of global warming.

I drink it every day.

IN 1907, Russian scientist Elie Metchnikoff noticed that many of his oldest—and healthiest—patients drank milk that had been turned sour by bacteria. He gave bacteria the credit and suggested that people eat foods with similar "good" bacteria.

Not sauerkraut again!

ENGLISH EXPLORER James Cook always packed sauerkraut on his long voyages. The vitamin C in the cabbage helped prevent the dangerous disease scurvy. But the cabbage doesn't keep unless it has been pickled and turned into sauerkraut—and you need bacteria to help do that pickling.

Can Dirt Be Good For You?

Some children's eyes would light up if they heard that the answer to that question is "yes." Of course, it's not that we should *never* wash ourselves, and wallow around in mud all the time. But it may be true that sometimes people take cleaning a little too far.

We need good bacteria to remain healthy. But a cleaning product that "kills all sorts of germs" kills both good and bad bacteria. So your hands, or kitchen range, or bathtub will look bright and clean, but you might lose some of those good bacteria along the way. That's a problem that scientists are now beginning to study, to see if being "too clean" can make you a bit sick.

IT MIGHT BE GOOD FOR YOU to become exposed to different bacteria while you're young. Your body will either learn to live with them or build up defenses. Maybe playing with your family pooch now will help you to be healthier when you're older.

18

SCIENTISTS HAVE linked one strain of bacteria in ordinary soil to the release of serotonin. That's a chemical that makes you feel happy. But it's still a good idea to wash your hands because of other bacteria in soil.

You Can Do It!

If you spread a spoonful of garden soil on a piece of paper and look at it with a magnifying glass, you'll probably see tiny living creatures. But if you use a powerful microscope, you'll be able to see more than 100 million bacteria.

ALLERGIES are strong reactions to certain animals, fabrics, or foods. Some experts believe that allergies develop because people haven't had exposure to a range of bacteria—because everything today is too clean!

THIS CHILD has probably picked up a few million bacteria while playing outside. Some of these may strengthen his body's immune system and help him to fight off infections in the future.

MAGNETOSPIRILLUM bacteria are able to use iron particles to make the magnetic mineral magnetite. This allows them to align themselves with Earth's magnetic field—as if they were using the magnetite as a natural compass.

How Do Plants Use Bacteria?

Most plants make their own food using carbon dioxide from the air around them, and light. This process, called photosynthesis, keeps plants nourished and healthy. Nitrogen, another gas that plants need to thrive, is 200 times more plentiful than carbon dioxide in the air around you. But it's locked in a form that makes it hard to use.

That's where bacteria come to the rescue. They transform the nitrogen in the air into a form that plants can use. That process is called nitrogen fixation. Without this usable form of nitrogen, plants struggle to produce food through photosynthesis. When the plant dies, the "fixed" nitrogen enters the soil, to be used by other plants. This whole process is called the nitrogen cycle. Without those helpful bacteria, no life-forms would exist.

A SMART FARMER alternates crops in a field. One year he might grow legumes—plants that attract lots of nitrogen-fixing bacteria. They deposit plenty of good nitrogen in the soil, so that the corn or wheat grown there the next year will flourish.

NITROGEN turns plants into food factories, nourishing themselves and providing excellent harvests for farmers. Without nitrogen, fields can look withered and unhealthy.

THE NITROGEN ATOMS in the air are locked together. It's only when bacteria react with this nitrogen that it is changed to a form that plants can use.

And it's all thanks to something you can't even see!

Bumper crop this year!

How It Works

Nitrogen-fixing bacteria live in bulbs called nodules in the roots of legumes. Legumes include clover, beans, and peanuts. The plants provide energy to help the bacteria convert nitrogen from the air into the form that the plants can use.

Nodules

A FARMER who hasn't grown legumes to encourage bacteria will need to use fertilizer to make sure that the crops receive enough nitrogen. But fertilizers are expensive, so many farmers prefer the natural approach—letting the bacteria do the work for free.

EVERYONE WINS when bacteria team up with plants in the nitrogen cycle. The plants receive nitrogen in a form that they can use to produce food. In return, the bacteria receive food and oxygen from the plant—to help them release more nitrogen.

21

Is It Good That Things Break Down?

No one wants to have to wade through piles of dead plants and animals—and, thanks to bacteria, we don't have to. Along with other microorganisms, bacteria eat away at dead material.

But that's not the end of the story. Those dead things haven't just disappeared—the bacteria have broken them up into different parts. And many of those ingredients are nutrients that return to the soil and enrich it. Richer soil means better conditions for more plants to grow, and having more plants around makes life better for animals. You're one of those animals, so remember to thank the invisible bacteria next time you toss a banana peel into a compost pile.

1. DON'T THROW IT AWAY! You can put some kinds of food waste in a compost maker (below). That's a special outdoor container, where the food breaks down to become compost—a natural fertilizer. Bacteria have a starring role in that process, but they're helped out by worms and insects, and by other microorganisms.

1

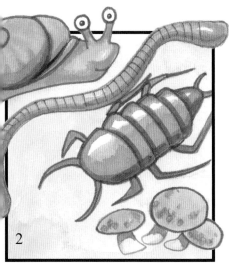

2. SNAILS, SLUGS, worms, insects, and fungi all join in the feast if the temperature and amount of air reaching the compost are right (top left).

3. ONCE THE BACTERIA and other tiny creatures have done their work, the result is a natural fertilizer that is easy to mix into soil (middle left). This compost is full of nutrients to help plants grow.

You Can Do It!

Why not create your own compost maker? Start with an old plastic trash can. Poke holes all around it and on the lid. Fill it with peels and eggshells, but not meat or fish (so you don't encourage unwelcome pests). Use a strong rake or garden fork to turn it regularly. The compost should be damp but not wet.

4. SMALL ANIMALS OFTEN shelter in compost or bonfire piles in cold weather, because heat is released as bacteria break down organic material (bottom left). If an adult is lighting a fire, have him or her check first that there are no animals snuggled inside.

WHERE AN ANIMAL DIES, and under what conditions, determines how long it will take to decompose, or be broken down (above right). A dead rat in a crowded forest might take just a couple of days, but a dead whale on the cold ocean floor will take up to 16 years to become a skeleton.

AMMONIA and other smelly gases are released as bacteria break down the cells of dead animals (below). Sometimes gas can build up inside the animal, and even cause it to explode.

Let's get out of here!

Is Waste Always Wasteful?

It's great to think that you can put some of your household waste to work by creating compost so you can grow plants. But imagine being able to take all of a city's waste and putting it to use. That's exactly what is happening in many parts of the world, and, as usual, bacteria are helping out.

Everyone benefits from projects that put bacteria to work. Cities find ways of dealing with waste before it builds up into smelly mountains. The bacteria get a permanent supply of food. And then there are some unexpected side effects. Could anyone have predicted that we'd be able to use garbage to generate electricity? Scientists are constantly learning more about how to work with bacteria.

OIL SPILLS can cause lasting damage to oceans and coastlines. But some bacteria treat the floating oil as food. With the right planning, bacteria can be brought in to eat up the oil, and then to become food for sea creatures.

FARMERS have used bacteria to feed their cattle for nearly 200 years. Silage is made from bits of corn, oats, and clover that have fermented—and it's bacteria that trigger that fermenting.

CELL PHONE BATTERIES might one day be recharged using urine. Scientists have combined bacteria and urine to produce an electrical charge that could be used in phones.

BACTERIA'S APPETITE for what we call waste is astounding. Scientists have even modified one species of bacteria so that it can consume and digest poisons in nuclear waste.

CENTURIES AGO, people dumped sewage onto the street or into pipes that fed straight into rivers and lakes. Modern sewage treatment systems often use bacteria that feed on the waste. Some of the by-products can be useful to humans.

How It Works

As bacteria digest the waste in sewage treatment plants, they produce large amounts of methane. This is a gas that burns very well, but can increase global warming if it escapes into the atmosphere. Some plants trap the gas so that it can be burned in order to produce electricity.

The sewage tanks don't smell at all!

That's because of the special aluminum covers.

Do Industries Use Bacteria?

As scientists, doctors, and engineers constantly observe new benefits from bacteria, new industries are following right behind them.

Companies are finding new ways of harnessing the power and possibilities of bacteria—and creating jobs at the same time. And those jobs are developing in all sorts of areas, from farming to energy production—and even reaching the world of fashion. Maybe bacteria will eventually help us all to reduce our reliance on gasoline, oil, and other fossil fuels.

The Future of Food?

GENETIC MODIFICATION means altering the DNA of an organism, which contains the information that living things pass on to their offspring. For example, scientists have found disease-fighting genes in bacteria. The scientists can add these genes to plants, which can then fight those diseases—and pass on the new genes to their offspring.

Healthy corn—thanks to the bacteria!

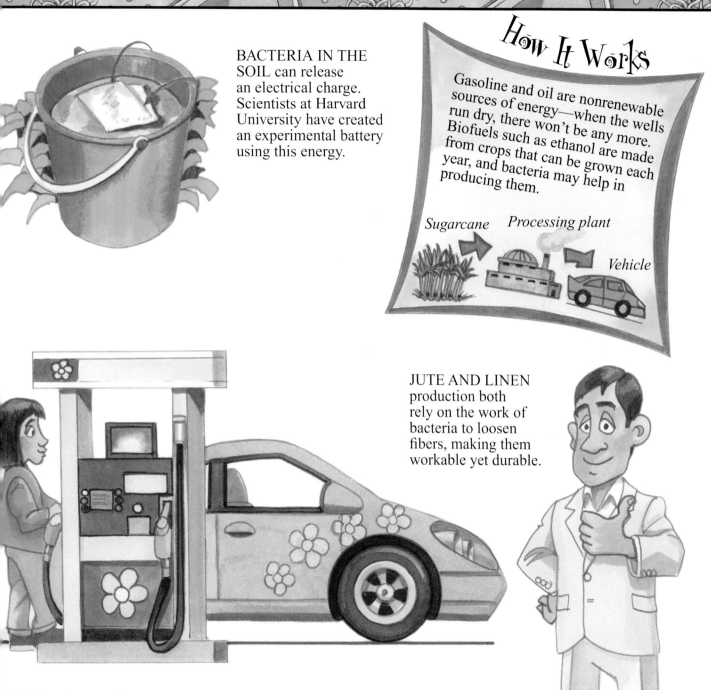

BACTERIA IN THE SOIL can release an electrical charge. Scientists at Harvard University have created an experimental battery using this energy.

How It Works

Gasoline and oil are nonrenewable sources of energy—when the wells run dry, there won't be any more. Biofuels such as ethanol are made from crops that can be grown each year, and bacteria may help in producing them.

Sugarcane   *Processing plant*

Vehicle

JUTE AND LINEN production both rely on the work of bacteria to loosen fibers, making them workable yet durable.

ETHANOL, a fuel made from the natural sugar in corn or sugarcane, could help replace fossil fuels such as gasoline and diesel. But corn and sugarcane are useful food crops. Scientists are now experimenting with new forms of bacteria that can produce the right kind of sugar more quickly and at less cost, without using up valuable food crops. Some of these bacteria use the energy in sunlight to produce the sugars that are used to make ethanol.

What Lies Ahead?

We've made great strides in the few centuries since bacteria were first identified. We've discovered that some can be deadly killers, while others are friendly neighbors, and we've learned how these one-celled organisms live and reproduce. The future seems bright, with scientists constantly finding new ways to use bacteria in medicine, cooking, industry, and transportation. The next few decades could see us using bacteria to tackle some of our toughest problems—possibly providing cures for deadly diseases, providing "green" energy, and making our planet cleaner for those who come after us.

ONE PROMISING AREA of bacteria study is cancer treatment. Some kinds of *Clostridium* bacteria are able to survive inside a cancer tumor, even though there is no oxygen there. The bacteria may be able to deliver cancer-destroying medicines right into the tumor.

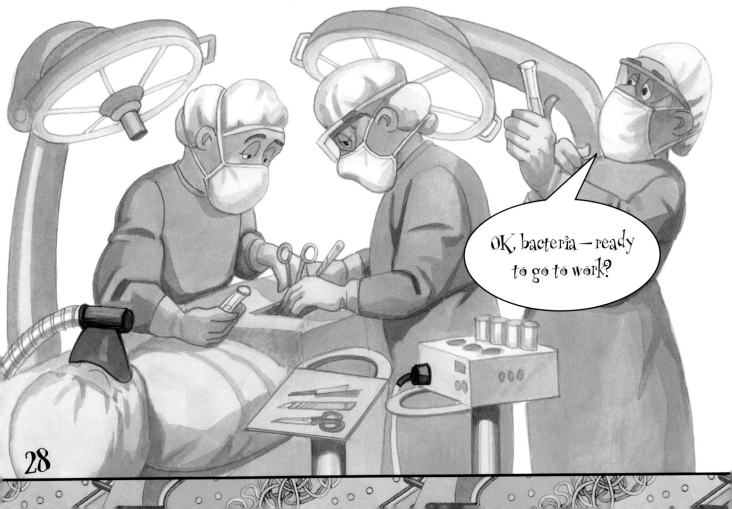

AIR POLLUTION, caused largely by vehicles and industries, is a serious problem in many cities. Maybe bacteria could help get rid of some of the unhealthy material floating in the air. Scientists have already observed how bacteria high in Earth's atmosphere produce chemicals that react with—and consume—pollutants.

You Can Do It!

Draw up a list of areas where you think bacteria will make a big difference in the future. Which do you think is the most important—industry, farming, cooking? Might there be other areas that no one's thought of yet?

Rocket fuel!?

NITROGEN from fertilizers can seep into rivers and flow into the ocean, where it helps algae to grow. Other sea organisms can't survive under this blanket of algae. But bacteria can be used to react with the nitrogen and send it harmlessly into the atmosphere.

IT IS DIFFICULT to extract valuable minerals from ores which contain only small amounts of the minerals. But biomining involves soaking ore in acid and then adding bacteria. The bacteria react with the mixture, releasing pure metal in the process.

Food supplements

Yogurt

Soy protein

SOMETIMES the "good" bacteria in your intestines—which fight infection and help you digest food—need some help. They don't work as well as you get older, for example. Some "smart foods" may provide an extra supply of these helpful bacteria.

Glossary

biofuel A fuel made from an organism that can be grown.

by-product Something that is produced in the process of producing something else.

cell A tiny part of an organism, having a nucleus (center) and a cell membrane.

compost A mixture of decayed organisms, used to enrich soil.

decompose To decay and break down into simpler ingredients.

digestive system All the parts of the body that work together to break down food so that it can be used as energy.

DNA The genetic code of an organism, containing information that is passed on to its offspring.

dormant Not active, but able to become active again.

enzyme A chemical produced by a plant or animal to help digestion or other activities.

ethanol A type of alcohol, often used as a fuel, produced from natural sugars.

ferment To change a sugar chemically into alcohol and carbon dioxide.

food cycle The process by which organisms eat other organisms and are eaten in turn.

fossil fuel A source of energy coming from material that was alive long ago—as coal and oil were once plants.

fungus (plural **fungi**) An organism that is neither plant, animal, nor bacterium. Yeast and mushrooms are fungi.

genetic Relating to genes, the part of a cell that controls the growth, appearance, and reproduction of a living thing.

germ A general term to describe bacteria, viruses, and other tiny organisms.

global warming A rise in the temperature of Earth's atmosphere, caused by gases and other substances (some of them produced by humans) that prevent heat from escaping.

immune system The body's network of cells, chemicals, and organs that it uses to fight disease.

infection An invasion of the body by organisms that cause disease.

microbe or **microorganism** Any tiny living organism that is too small to see with the naked eye.

nutrient Anything that provides food.

ore Rock that contains a valuable substance, usually a metal.

organism Any living thing.

parasite An organism that lives on or in another organism and gets nourishment from it.

pasteurization A method of heating food or drink to kill off harmful bacteria and other microorganisms. It was invented by French scientist Louis Pasteur.

pollutant A substance that enters the air, water, or soil, making it unsafe or dirty.

protein A chemical building block of tissue.

react To change chemically upon coming in contact with another substance.

scurvy A disease, now rare, that can lead to weakness, loss of teeth, and heart problems.

sewage Human waste that is flushed away from homes or other buildings.

tuberculosis A lung disease caused by bacteria.

tumor An uncontrolled growth in the body, caused by diseases such as cancer.

viruses Tiny organisms that resemble bacteria in some ways but cannot reproduce by themselves. Instead, viruses infect cells in other organisms and reproduce when the infected cells reproduce.

Index

Bacteria and Disease

Though the vast majority of bacteria are either harmless or even helpful to humans, some of the "bad" bacteria can be deadly.

Doctors describe wide-ranging outbreaks of disease as pandemics. In the past, tens or even hundreds of millions of people have died in pandemics. And bacteria were responsible for several of the diseases, such as the plague, that led to these pandemics. Other deadly bacterial diseases, such as tuberculosis and cholera, have done their work more steadily throughout history.

In addition to these killer diseases, bacteria can cause illnesses and infections that range from those that are only annoying to those that need urgent hospital treatment. Because bacteria are so adaptable, the range of these conditions is staggering. Some bacteria, for example, can survive without oxygen. They can get to work even inside sealed spaces such as cans of food (though canned food is normally safe if the canning has been done properly and the can is not damaged). Others live in more open surroundings and wait to "catch a ride" into your body. *Clostridium tetani* bacteria, for example, live in soil, house dust, and animal waste. They can enter your body through a cut or burn. Once inside, they can cause a serious disease called tetanus, which affects your nervous system and muscles.

Luckily, cases of tetanus are very rare. That's because most countries have programs of vaccination—injecting children regularly with a weakened form of the disease, which allows the body's own immune system to prepare its defenses. If your shots are up to date, then you won't contract tetanus.

The treatment for tetanus relies largely on a type of drug called antibiotics. The name refers to the fact that the drug is fighting against ("anti") a biological enemy (the bacteria). Penicillin was the first really successful antibiotic drug to be developed. It was created after Sir Alexander Fleming noticed by chance that a mold or fungus called *Penicillium* was able to kill bacteria. Over the years, penicillin and other antibiotics have been used to prevent or treat many bacterial illnesses.

Your body's immune system can fight off less dangerous infections by itself. It does this by creating substances called antibodies, which attack the bacteria. Some antibodies remain in the body afterward, so that if the same illness strikes again, you have a better chance of overcoming it quickly. Doctors describe that as developing immunity to a disease.

Using antibiotics too often can be bad for you. Bacteria can build up a resistance to the antibiotics, which means that the medicine is no longer effective against them.

This is why, when your doctor gives you antibiotics, you must keep taking them until you have finished them all. If you stop taking them as soon as you start to feel better, some of the bacteria may survive inside you — and they will be resistant to the antibiotic. Medical scientists fight a constant battle to develop new types of antibiotics to keep one step ahead of this defense by bacteria.

Top Three Plague Attacks

The Plague of Justinian (541–542 CE): This was the first recorded attack of the disease, during the reign of Emperor Justinian I of the Eastern Roman Empire. Continued outbreaks over the next two centuries killed more than 100 million people living near the Mediterranean Sea.

The Black Death (1346–1353): Sometimes called simply the Great Plague, this outbreak spread west from Asia and killed up to 60 percent of the people in some European countries.

3. **The Modern Plague** (1894–1914): Developing in China in the 1860s, this outbreak became far worse when it reached Hong Kong in 1894. Over the next 20 years more than 10 million people died worldwide.

Did You Know?

The word *bacterium* comes from the Greek *bakterion* (small stick or rod), because that's what the first bacteria that people saw looked like.

There are more bacteria in your intestines than there are people on Earth.

- The pleasant smell of rain is caused when water reaches *Actinomycetes* bacteria, which live in the soil.

- Human sweat has no odor, until it comes into contact with bacteria that live on the skin.